GOOGLE CLOUD PLATFORM

LEARN GOOGLE CLOUD PLATFORM FROM THE SCRATCH

ADNEY AINSLEY

Table of Contents

CHAPTER 1: CREATING AN INSTANCE

AWS vs GCP

"If you are familiar with Amazon Web Services (AWS), a quick way to understand what the various Google Cloud Platform (GCP) services do is to map them to AWS services that offer similar functionality. The following table provides a high-level mapping of the services provided by the two platforms" - Map AWS services to Google Cloud Platform products.

Service Category	Service	AWS	Google Cloud Platform
Compute	IaaS	Amazon Elastic Compute Cloud	Compute Engine
	PaaS	AWS Elastic Beanstalk	App Engine
	Containers	Amazon Elastic Compute Cloud Container Service	Google Kubernetes Engine
	Serverless Functions	AWS Lambda	Cloud Functions
	Managed Batch Computing	AWS Batch	N/A
Network	Virtual Networks	Amazon Virtual Private Cloud	Virtual Private Cloud
	Load Balancer	Elastic Load Balancer	Cloud Load Balancing
	Dedicated Interconnect	Direct Connect	Cloud Interconnect
	Domains and DNS	Amazon Route 53	Google Domains, Cloud DNS
	CDN	Amazon CloudFront	Cloud Content Delivery Network
Storage	Object Storage	Amazon Simple Storage Service	Cloud Storage
	Block Storage	Amazon Elastic Block Store	Persistent Disk
	Reduced-availability Storage	Amazon S3 Standard-Infrequent Access, Amazon S3 One Zone-Infrequent Access	Cloud Storage Nearline
	Archival Storage	Amazon Glacier	Cloud Storage Coldline

	File Storage	Amazon Elastic File System	Cloud Filestore (beta)
Database	RDBMS	Amazon Relational Database Service, Amazon Aurora	Cloud SQL, Cloud Spanner
	NoSQL: Key-value	Amazon DynamoDB	Cloud Datastore, Cloud Bigtable
	NoSQL: Indexed	Amazon SimpleDB	Cloud Datastore
Big Data & Analytics	Batch Data Processing	Amazon Elastic MapReduce, AWS Batch	Cloud Dataproc, Cloud Dataflow
	Stream Data Processing	Amazon Kinesis	Cloud Dataflow
	Stream Data Ingest	Amazon Kinesis	Cloud Pub/Sub
	Analytics	Amazon Redshift, Amazon Athena	BigQuery
	Workflow Orchestration	Amazon Data Pipeline, AWS Glue	Cloud Composer
Application Services	Messaging	Amazon Simple Notification Service, Amazon Simple Queueing Service	Cloud Pub/Sub
Management Services	Monitoring	Amazon CloudWatch	Stackdriver Monitoring
	Logging	Amazon CloudWatch Logs	Stackdriver Logging
	Deployment	AWS CloudFormation	Cloud Deployment Manager
Machine Learning	Speech	Amazon Transcribe	Cloud Speech-to-Text API

Creating a Linux VM instance

In this section, we'll create a Linux virtual machine instance in Compute Engine using the Google Cloud Platform Console.

1. Create a GCP project from Google Cloud Platform console.

Select a project   **NEW PROJECT**

Q Search projects and folders

RECENT   ALL

Name   ID

• LinuxVM ⊘   linuxvm-216022

2. Go to the VM instances page.

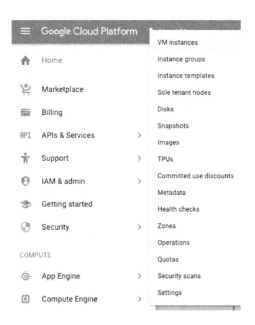

3. Click Create instance.
4. In the Boot disk section, click Change to begin configuring our boot disk.
5. In the OS images tab, choose Debian 9.

Select Show images with Shielded VM features to see only Shielded VM images.

Boot disk

Select an image or snapshot to create a boot disk; or attach an existing disk

OS images   Application images   Custom images   Snapshots   Existing disks

---

ℹ️ Shielded VM is in Beta. Learn more   **Dismiss**

✓ Show images with Shielded VM features ⓘ

◉ 🔧 **Ubuntu 18.04 LTS**
Secure Boot ready, amd64 bionic image built on 2018-08-14

○ 🔧 **Container-Optimized OS 69-10895.52.0 beta**
Kernel: ChromiumOS-4.14.65 Kubernetes: 1.11.1 Docker: 17.03.2, Secure Boot ready

○ 🔧 **Container-Optimized OS 70-11021.11.0 dev**
Kernel: ChromiumOS-4.14.67 Kubernetes: 1.11.1 Docker: 18.06.1, Secure Boot ready

○ 🔧 **Container-Optimized OS 68-10718.102.0 stable**
Kernel: ChromiumOS-4.14.65 Kubernetes: 1.10.5 Docker: 17.03.2, Secure Boot ready

○ 🔧 **Windows Server version 1709 Datacenter Core**
Server Core, GPT, Secure Boot ready, x64 built on 20180814

○ 🔧 **Windows Server version 1803 Datacenter Core**
Server Core, GPT, Secure Boot ready, x64 built on 20180814

○ 🔧 **Windows Server 2012 R2 Datacenter Core**
Server Core, GPT, Secure Boot ready, x64 built on 20180814

○ 🔧 **Windows Server 2012 R2 Datacenter**
Server with Desktop Experience, GPT, Secure Boot ready, x64 built on 20180814

○ 🔧 **Windows Server 2016 Datacenter Core**
Server Core, GPT, Secure Boot ready, x64 built on 20180814

○ 🔧 **Windows Server 2016 Datacenter**
Server with Desktop Experience, GPT, Secure Boot ready, x64 built on 20180814

Can't find what you're looking for? Explore hundreds of VM solutions in Marketplace

Boot disk type ⓘ	Size (GB) ⓘ
Standard persistent disk ▾	10

Select   Cancel

---

6.   Click Select.
7.   In the Firewall section, select Allow HTTP traffic. The GCP Console adds a network tag to our instance and creates the corresponding ingress firewall rule that allows all incoming traffic on tcp:80 (HTTP) or tcp:443 (HTTPS). The network tag associates the firewall rule with the instance.

Create an instance

micro (1 shared... ▾)   0.6 GB memory   Customize

Container
Deploy a container image to this VM instance. Learn more

Boot disk

New 10 GB standard persistent disk

Image

🐧 Ubuntu 18.04 LTS   Change

Identity and API access

Service account
Compute Engine default service account   ▾

Access scopes
● Allow default access
○ Allow full access to all Cloud APIs
○ Set access for each API

Firewall
Add tags and firewall rules to allow specific network traffic from the Internet
✓ Allow HTTP traffic
☐ Allow HTTPS traffic

⌄ Management, security, disks, networking, sole tenancy

You will be billed for this instance. Learn more

[Create]   Cancel

Equivalent REST or command line

8. Click Create to create the instance.

Connecting to Instances

Compute Engine provides tools to manage our SSH keys and help us connect to either Linux.

We can connect to Linux instances through either the Google Cloud Platform Console or the gcloud command-line tool. Compute Engine generates an SSH key for us and stores it in one of the following locations:

1. By default, Compute Engine adds the generated key to project or instance metadata.
2. If our account is configured to use OS Login, Compute Engine stores the generated key with our user account.
3. In the list of virtual machine instances, click SSH in the row of the instance that we want to connect to.
4. After we connect, we can use the terminal to run commands on our Linux instance.

5. When we are done, use the 'exit' command to disconnect from the instance.

CHAPTER 2: CREATING WINDOWS INSTANCES

Creating a Windows Server instance

Compute Engine provides public images with Windows Server that you can use to create instances.

Note: Windows Server images are premium resources that incur additional fees to use.

To create an instance with Windows Server, specify the image family for the specific version of Windows that you need. Compute Engine offers several versions of Windows Server, most of which are available as Shielded VM images.

Shielded VM images offer security features like UEFI-compliant firmware, Secure Boot, and vTPM-protected Measured Boot.

Note: All Windows Server instances must be able to communicate with kms.windows.googlecloud.com (35.190.247.13/32) to activate its license.

To create a basic Windows instance:

1. In the Cloud Console, go to the VM Instances page.
2. Click Create instance.
3. In the Boot disk section, click Change to begin configuring your boot disk.
4. On the Public images tab, choose a Windows image.
5. Click Select.
6. Click Create to create the instance.

To create a Shielded VM Windows instance:

1. Go to the VM instances page.
2. Click Create instance.
3. In the Boot disk section, click Change to begin configuring your boot disk.

4. In the Public images tab, choose Windows Server operating system version.
   To see only the Shielded VM images, select Show images with Shielded VM features.
5. Click Save to save your boot disk configuration.
6. Optionally, change the instance's Shielded VM settings:

   a) Click on the Security tab in the Management Security Disks Networking section.
   b) If you want to disable Secure Boot, uncheck Turn on Secure Boot. Secure Boot helps protect your VM instances against boot-level and kernel-level malware and rootkits.
   c) If you want to disable the virtual trusted platform module (vTPM), uncheck Turn on vTPM. The vTPM enables Measured Boot, which validates the VM pre-boot and boot integrity.
   d) Important: Disabling the vTPM also disables integrity monitoring, because integrity monitoring relies on data gathered by Measured Boot.
   e) If you want to disable integrity monitoring, uncheck Turn on Integrity Monitoring. Integrity monitoring lets you monitor the boot integrity of your Shielded VM instances using Cloud Monitoring
   f) Click Create to create the instance.

7. After you create your Windows or SQL Server instance, set the initial password for the instance so that you can connect to the instance through RDP.

Creating a Windows Server instance that uses an internal IP address to activate

Before you can create a Windows Server instance that has only an internal IP address, you must verify or configure routes and firewall rules in your VPC network to allow access to kms.windows.googlecloud.com. Additionally, you must enable Private Google Access for subnets in your VPC network that contain Windows instances with only internal IP addresses.

When you create a new instance by using the gcloud command line, you can use the --no-address flag to ensure that it is not assigned an external IP address:

```
gcloud compute instances create [INSTANCE_NAME] --network [NETWORK_NAME] \
    --subnet [SUBNET_NAME] \
    --no-address \
    --zone [ZONE] \
    --image-project windows-cloud \
    --image-family [IMAGE_FAMILY] \
    --machine-type [MACHINE_TYPE] \
    --boot-disk-size [BOOT_DISK_SIZE] \
    --boot-disk-type [BOOT_DISK_TYPE]
```

Replace the following placeholders with valid values:

❖ [INSTANCE_NAME] is the name for the new instance.

❖ [SUBNET_NAME] is the name of the subnet in the VPC network that the instance will use. The subnet must be in the same region as the zone you choose for the instance.

❖ [IMAGE_FAMILY] is one of the public image families for Windows Server images.

❖ [MACHINE_TYPE] is one of the available machine types.

❖ [BOOT_DISK_SIZE] is the size of the boot disk in GB. Larger persistent disks have higher throughput.

❖ [BOOT_DISK_TYPE] is the type of the boot disk for your instance. For example, pd-ssd.

Because this instance does not have an external IP address, you cannot connect to it directly over the Internet. You can connect from another network connected to your VPC network by using Cloud Interconnect or Cloud VPN, or you can first connect to a bastion instance over RDP and then connect to the instance that has only an internal IP address.

Configuring access to kms.windows.googlecloud.com

For Windows activation and renewal, your VPC network must meet the following routing and firewall rule requirements.

Routing requirements

Your Windows instances must be able to reach kms.windows.googlecloud.com (35.190.247.13) through a route whose next hop is the default Internet gateway. You cannot activate Windows instances using an instance based NAT gateway or Cloud NAT because kms.windows.googlecloud.com rejects activation requests from IP addresses that are not confirmed to be Compute Engine instances.

You can use the default route in your VPC network to route traffic directly to kms.windows.googlecloud.com. If you remove this route, or if you plan to do so in the future, create a custom static route with destination 35.190.247.13 and next hop set to default Internet gateway:

```
gcloud compute routes create [ROUTE_NAME] \
    --destination-range=35.190.247.13/32 \
    --network=[NETWORK] \
    --next-hop-gateway=default-internet-gateway
```

Replace [ROUTE_NAME] with a name for this route and [NETWORK] with the name of your VPC network.

Either the default route or a custom static route as described above will permit instances with external IP addresses to reach kms.windows.googlecloud.com. If you have Windows instances without external IP addresses, you must also enable Private Google Access so that instances with only internal IP addresses can send traffic to the external IP address for kms.windows.googlecloud.com. That IP address, 35.190.247.13, is included in the list of IP addresses for Google APIs and services.

Firewall rule requirements

The implied allow egress firewall rule allows instances to make requests and receive established responses. Unless you have created custom firewall rules that deny egress, your Windows instances can communicate with kms.windows.googlecloud.com.

If you customize firewall rules, it's a good practice to create a high priority egress allow rule that explicitly permits communication with 35.190.247.13. This way, as you modify your firewall rules, you won't accidentally disable Windows activation.

The following gcloud examples creates the recommended allow egress rule with the highest priority:

```
gcloud compute firewall-rules create [RULE_NAME] \
    --direction=EGRESS \
    --network=[NETWORK] \
    --action=ALLOW \
    --rules=tcp:1688 \
    --destination-ranges=35.190.247.13/32 \
    --priority=0
```

Replace [RULE_NAME] with a name for this firewall rule and [NETWORK] with the name of your VPC network.

Verifying that an instance has successfully started

Windows instances experience a longer startup time because of the sysprep process. The Cloud Console might show that the instance is running even if the sysprep process is not yet complete. To check if your instance has successfully started and is ready to be used, check the serial port output with the following command:

```
gcloud compute instances get-serial-port-output [INSTANCE_NAME]
```

where [INSTANCE_NAME] is the name of the instance you want to verify.

```
...[snip]...
Running schtasks with arguments /run /tn GCEStartup
-->  SUCCESS: Attempted to run the scheduled task "GCEStartup".
-------------------------------------------------------------
Instance setup finished. [INSTANCE_NAME] is ready to use.
-------------------------------------------------------------
```

Disabling Google-provided component updates

If you have Windows instances with image versions v20170509 and later or with agent version 4.1.0 and later, Google-provided components such as the agent, metadata, and sysprep scripts are updated automatically using a scheduled task. The scheduled task is set up by the google-compute-engine-auto-updater package.

If you want to manage updates manually or manage updates using an alternative system you can disable these automatic component updates by removing the google-compute-engine-auto-updater package:

1. On the Windows Server instance, open a PowerShell terminal as an administrator.
2. Run the googet remove command to remove the package:

```
PS C:\\> googet remove google-compute-engine-auto-updater
```

Optionally, you can reinstall the package to enable automatic component updates:

1. On the Windows Server instance, open a PowerShell terminal as an administrator.
2. Run the googet install command to install the package:

```
PS C:\\> googet install google-compute-engine-auto-updater
```

Alternatively, you can disable the updates by setting the disable-agent-updates value to true in project or instance custom metadata. The metadata value disables updates without removing the package or the task.

Enabling and disabling Windows instance features

If you have Windows instances with image versions v20170509 and later or with agent version 4.1.0 and later, you can set instance configuration in a config file or in project or instance custom metadata. The config file is in INI format, and is located at the following path:

```
C:\Program Files\Google\Compute Engine\instance_configs.cfg
```

The system overrides configuration settings in the following order of priority from the highest priority to the lowest priority:

1. Configuration parameters that you set in the config file
2. Configuration parameters set in instance-level custom metadata
3. Configuration parameters set in project-level custom metadata

For example, if you can enable the accountManager feature in a config file, your instance ignores parameters that you set in custom metadata to disable that feature.

One benefit of setting these parameters in the config file is that those settings persist when you create a custom image for a Windows Server instance. Instance-level custom metadata does not persist beyond the life of the instance.

You can disable different Windows instance features using the following examples:

Disable the account manager, which also disables resetting passwords with the gcloud command-line tool or the Console:

❖ Config file:

```
[accountManager]
disable=true
```

❖ In custom metadata, set disable-account-manager to true in metadata.

Disable the address manager:

❖ Config file entry:

```
[addressManager]
disable=tru
```

```
[addressManager]
disable=true
```

❖ In custom metadata, set disable-address-manager to true in metadata.

Windows Server Failover Clustering

Enable the Windows Server Failover Clustering agent:

❖ Config file entry:

```
[wsfc]
enable=true
```

❖   In custom metadata, set enable-wsfc to true in metadata.

Using multiple internal load balancers

Specify the IP address of the internal load balancing instance for failover clustering. This is an advanced configuration that you don't need to set for a dedicated failover cluster.

Normally you use an instance of internal load balancing to direct network traffic to one VM instance at a time. If you add a second instance of internal load balancing that uses the failover clustering VM instances as part of a load-balanced website backend, you would have two internal load balancing IP addresses. If failover clustering uses 10.0.0.10 and the website's load balancer uses 10.0.0.11, you must specify the IP address of the load balancer that you use for failover clustering. This disambiguates which address is in use for the cluster.

❖   Config file entry:

```
[wsfc]
addresses=10.0.0.10|
```

❖   In custom metadata, set wsfc-addrs to a 10.0.0.10.

Changing the clustering agent port

Set the failover clustering agent port. The default port is 59998. You need to specify a port only when you want to use a different port:

❖   Config file entry:

```
[wsfc]
port=12345
```

❖ In custom metadata, set wsfc-agent-port to the port number.

Image version notes

Older images do not use a config file and only have a subset of features. Image versions between version v20160112 and version v20170509, or Windows agent version between 3.2.1.0 and 4.0.0 require you to use the following custom metadata values:

❖ Set disable-account-manager to true in instance metadata to disable the account manager.

❖ Set disable-address-manager to true in instance metadata to disable the address manager.

CHAPTER 3: GCLOUD COMPUTE COMMAND-LINE TOOL

gcloud compute command-line tool

The gcloud compute command-line tool enables us to easily manage our Google Compute Engine resources in a friendlier format than using the Compute Engine API.

The gcloud tool is part of the Cloud SDK and is a unified command-line tool that includes features like statement autocompletion, in-place updating, extensive man page style help, human-readable and machine-parsable output formats, and integration with Google Cloud SDK - gcloud compute

Setup gcloud compute

Google Compute Engine uses OAuth2 to authenticate and authorize access. Before we can use gcloud compute, we must first authorize the Cloud SDK on our behalf to access our project and acquire an auth token.

If we are using the gcloud command-line tool for the first time, gcloud automatically uses the default configuration. For most cases, we only need the default configuration.

1. Run gcloud init to start the authentication process. Hit enter when prompted. The command prints a URL and tries to open a browser window to request access to our project. If a browser window can be opened, we will see the following output:

```
$ gcloud init
Welcome! This command will take you through the configuration of
gcloud.

Your current configuration has been set to: [default]

You can skip diagnostics next time by using the following flag:

  gcloud init --skip-diagnostics

Network diagnostic detects and fixes local network connection issues.

Checking network connection...done.

Reachability Check passed.

Network diagnostic (1/1 checks) passed.

You must log in to continue. Would you like to log in (Y/n)?  Y

Your browser has been opened to visit:


https://accounts.google.com/o/oauth2/auth?redirect_uri=http%3A%2F%2Flo
calhost%3A8085%2F&prompt=select_account&response_type=code&client_id=3
2555940559.apps.googleusercontent.com&scope=https%3A%2F%2Fwww.googleap
is.com%2Fauth%2Fuserinfo.email+https%3A%2F%2Fwww.googleapis.com%2Fauth
%2Fcloud-
platform+https%3A%2F%2Fwww.googleapis.com%2Fauth%2Fappengine.admin+htt
ps%3A%2F%2Fwww.googleapis.com%2Fauth%2Fcompute+https%3A%2F%2Fwww.googl
eapis.com%2Fauth%2Faccounts.reauth&access_type=offline
```

G Sign in with Google

Choose an account

to continue to Google Cloud SDK

@gmail.com

🧑 Use another account

To continue, Google will share your name, email address,
and profile picture with Google Cloud SDK.

English (United States) ▾   Help   Privacy   Terms

G Sign in with Google

Google Cloud SDK wants to access your Google Account

[   ]@gmail.com

This will allow Google Cloud SDK **to:**

- View and manage your applications deployed on (i) Google App Engine

- View and manage your Google Compute Engine (i) resources

- View and manage your data across Google Cloud (i) Platform services

Make sure you trust Google Cloud SDK

You may be sharing sensitive info with this site or app. Learn about how Google Cloud SDK will handle your data by reviewing its terms of service and privacy policies. You can always see or remove access in your Google Account.

Learn about the risks

Cancel   Allow

```
You are logged in as: [sam.ple@gmail.com].
Pick cloud project to use:
 [1] djangotest-sfvue
 [2] epicmath-local
 [3] linuxvm-216022
 [4] mykubernetesproject-164618
 [5] pytato-142916
 [6] xophist-1248
 [7] youtubeinfo-1224
 [8] Create a new project
Please enter numeric choice or text value (must exactly match list
item):  3
```

Create instances

Use the instances create command to create a new instance. For example, the following command creates an instance named "my-instance" in the "us-central1-a" zone:

```
$ gcloud compute instances create my-instance
Created [https://www.googleapis.com/compute/v1/projects/linuxvm-
216022/zones/us-east1-c/instances/my-instance].
NAME          ZONE        MACHINE_TYPE    PREEMPTIBLE   INTERNAL_IP
EXTERNAL_IP    STATUS
my-instance  us-east1-c  n1-standard-1                 10.142.0.2
35.229.21.208  RUNNING
```

If we omit the "--zone" flag, gcloud can infer our desired zone based on our default   properties.

Other required instance settings, like machine type and image, if not specified in the create command, are set to default values. We can see the default values by displaying help for the create command:

```
$ gcloud compute instances create --help
```

To list instances:

```
$ gcloud compute instances list
NAME          ZONE        MACHINE_TYPE    PREEMPTIBLE   INTERNAL_IP
EXTERNAL_IP    STATUS
my-instance  us-east1-c  n1-standard-1                 10.142.0.2
35.229.21.208  RUNNING
```

Connecting to instances

The gcloud compute ssh command provides wrappers around around SSH, which takes care of authentication and the mapping of instance name to IP address.

to ssh in to "my-instance" in the "us-east1-c" zone, we can use:

```
$ gcloud compute ssh my-instance --zone us-east1-c
Updating project ssh metadata...⸮Updated [https://www.googleapis.com/compute/v1/projects/linuxvm-216022].
Updating project ssh metadata...done.
Waiting for SSH key to propagate.
Warning: Permanently added 'compute.4873874219097322680' (ECDSA) to the list of known hosts.
Linux my-instance 4.9.0-8-amd64 #1 SMP Debian 4.9.110-3+deb9u3 (2018-08-19) x86_64
The programs included with the Debian GNU/Linux system are free software;
the exact distribution terms for each program are described in the
individual files in /usr/share/doc/*/copyright.
Debian GNU/Linux comes with ABSOLUTELY NO WARRANTY, to the extent
permitted by applicable law.
sam.ple@my-instance:~$
```

To copy the local file "file-1" to "my-instance" in the "us-east1-c" zone, we can use:

```
$ gcloud compute scp ~/file-1 my-instance:~/test --zone us-east1-c
file-1
sam.ple@my-instance:~/test$ ls
file-1
```

The scp command can also be used to copy files from an instance to our local machine. For example, to create a local copy of "file-1", which is on the instance "my-instance" in the "us-east1-c" zone, we can use:

```
$ gcloud compute scp my-instance:~/test/file-2 ~/ --zone us-east1-c
file-2
```

Both the gcloud compute ssh and gcloud compute scp commands, by default, use the private key file located at "~/.ssh/google_compute_engine".

```
$ ls ~/.ssh
google_compute_engine          google_compute_engine.pub  google_compute_known_hosts known_hosts
```

Default zone and region

To set default zone and region in our local client. We can manually choose a different zone or region without updating the metadata server by setting these properties locally on our gcloud client.

We can change the default zone and region in our metadata server by making a request to the metadata server. For example:

```
$ gcloud compute project-info add-metadata \
    --metadata google-compute-default-region=us-east1,google-compute-default-zone=us-east1-c
Updated [https://www.googleapis.com/compute/v1/projects/linuxvm-216022].
```

CHAPTER 4: DEPLOYING CONTAINERS

Deploying Containers

We'll learn how to deploy Docker images on Google Compute Engine virtual machine instances.

To deploy and launch our container on a Compute Engine VM, we provide a Docker image name and configure how our container should run when creating a VM or an instance template. Compute Engine will take care of the rest including supplying an up-to-date Container-Optimized OS image with Docker installed and launching our container when the VM starts up.

Container-Optimized OS

Container-Optimized OS is an operating system image for our Compute Engine VMs that is optimized for running Docker containers. With Container-Optimized OS, we can bring up our Docker containers on Google Cloud Platform quickly, efficiently, and securely. Container-Optimized OS is maintained by Google and is based on the open source Chromium OS project.

Managed instance groups

A managed instance group uses an instance template to create a group of identical instances. We control a managed instance group as a single entity. If we wanted to make changes to instances that are part of a managed instance group, we would make the change to the whole instance group. Because managed instance groups contain identical instances, they offer the following features:

1. When our applications require additional compute resources, managed instance groups can automatically scale the number of instances in the group.
2. Managed instance groups work with load balancing services to distribute traffic to all of the instances in the group.
3. If an instance in the group stops, crashes, or is deleted by an action other than the instance groups commands, the managed instance group automatically recreates the instance so it can resume its

processing tasks. The recreated instance uses the same name and the same instance template as the previous instance, even if the group references a different instance template.

4. Managed instance groups can automatically identify and recreate unhealthy instances in a group to ensure that all of the instances are running optimally.

Deploy containers on VMs vs Kubernetes

Running each microservice on a separate VM on Compute Engine could make the operating system overhead a significant part of our cost. Kubernetes Engine allows us to deploy multiple containers and groups of containers for each VM instance, which can lead to more efficient host VM utilization for microservices with a smaller footprint.

We can only deploy one container for each VM instance. Consider Kubernetes Engine if we need to deploy multiple containers per VM instance.

Deploying a container on a managed instance group

We can deploy a container to a new managed instance group using Google Cloud Platform Console or the gcloud command line tool by following these steps:

1. Create an instance template, based on a Docker image.
2. Create a managed instance group from the new instance template.

We'll create an instance template that deploys a container from a Google-provided Nginx (gcr.io/cloud-marketplace/google/nginx1:1.12) Docker image to a managed instance group.

1. Go to the Instance templates page.

2. Click the "Create instance template" button to create a new instance template.

3. Under the Container section, check Deploy container image.

4. Specify the Docker image name under Container image and configure options to run the container if desired. For example, we can specify gcr.io/cloud-marketplace/google/nginx1:1.12 for the container image.

5. Click Create.

Now that we have an instance template, we can create a managed instance group using the instance template. For example, to create a managed instance group using the gcloud tool with the nginx-template that we just created, we need to run the following command:

```
$ gcloud compute instance-groups managed create example-group \
    --base-instance-name nginx-vm \
    --size 2 \
    --template instance-template-1
Created [https://www.googleapis.com/compute/v1/projects/linuxvm-216022/zones/us-east1-c/instanceGroupManagers/example-group].
NAME            LOCATION    SCOPE   BASE_INSTANCE_NAME  SIZE  TARGET_SIZE  INSTANCE_TEMPLATE    AUTOSCALED
example-group   us-east1-c  zone    nginx-vm            0     2            instance-template-1  no
```

Connecting to a container using SSH

We can connect to a container on a VM using SSH. In this case, use the gcloud beta compute ssh command instead of the standard gcloud compute ssh command. Using the gcloud tool, run the gcloud beta compute ssh command with the --container flag.

```
gcloud beta compute ssh [INSTANCE_NAME] --container [CONTAINER_NAME]
```

[INSTANCE_NAME] is the name of the VM instance.

[CONTAINER_NAME] is either the name of the standalone VM instance or the name of the instance template, if the instance belongs to a managed instance group.

```
$ gcloud beta compute ssh nginx-vm-1vxk --container instance-template-1
```

```
You do not currently have this command group installed. Using it
requires the installation of components: [beta]

Your current Cloud SDK version is: 215.0.0
Installing components from version: 215.0.0

┌─────────────────────────────────────────────────┐
│          These components will be installed.      │
├───────────────────────┬─────────────┬───────────┤
│         Name          │   Version   │    Size   │
├───────────────────────┼─────────────┼───────────┤
│ gcloud Beta Commands  │  2018.07.16 │   < 1 MiB │
└───────────────────────┴─────────────┴───────────┘

For the latest full release notes, please visit:
  https://cloud.google.com/sdk/release_notes

Do you want to continue (Y/n)?  y

╞═ Creating update staging area                    ═╡
╞═ Installing: gcloud Beta Commands                ═╡
╞═ Creating backup and activating new installation ═╡

Performing post processing steps...done.

Update done!

Restarting command:
  $ gcloud beta compute ssh nginx-vm-1vxk --container instance-template-1

Warning: Permanently added 'compute.2934697648299513574' (RSA) to the list of known hosts.
#
```

CHAPTER 5: KUBERNETES QUICKSTART

Kubernetes Quickstart

We'll learn how to deploy a containerized application with Kubernetes Engine.

1. Go to the Kubernetes Engine page in the Google Cloud Platform Console.

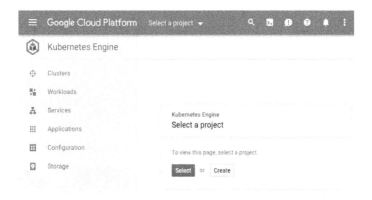

2. Create or select a project
3. Wait for the API and related services to be enabled. Create or select a project.

Kubernetes Engine is getting ready. This may take a minute or more. Kubernetes Engine documentation

This can take several minutes.

Google Cloud Shell

To complete this quickstart, we can use either Google Cloud Shell or our local shell. In this page, we'll use Google Cloud Shell.

Google Cloud Shell is a shell environment for managing resources hosted on Google Cloud Platform (GCP). Cloud Shell comes preinstalled with the gcloud and kubectl command-line tools. gcloud provides the primary command-line interface for GCP, and kubectl provides the command-line interface for running commands against Kubernetes clusters.

To launch Cloud Shell, perform the following steps:

1. Go to Google Cloud Platform Console.
2. From the top-right corner of the console, click the Activate Google Cloud Shell button:

A Cloud Shell session opens inside a frame at the bottom of the console.

We use this shell to run gcloud and kubectl commands.

Configuring default settings for gcloud

Before getting started, we should use gcloud to configure two default settings: our default project and compute zone.

Our project has a project ID, which is its unique identifier. When we first create a project, we can use the automatically-generated project ID or we can create our own.

Our compute zone is an approximate regional location in which our clusters and their resources live. For example, us-east1-a is a zone in the us-east region.

Configuring these default settings makes it easier to run gcloud commands, since gcloud requires that we specify the project and compute zone in which we wish to work. We can also specify these settings or override default settings by passing operational flags, such as --project, --zone, and --cluster, to gcloud commands.

When we create Kubernetes Engine resources after configuring our default project and compute zone, the resources are automatically created in that project and zone.

Setting a default project

To set a default project, run the following command from Cloud Shell:

```
gcloud config set project PROJECT_ID
kihyuck_hong@cloudshell:~ (kubernetesquickstart)$ gcloud config set project kubernetesquickstart
Updated property [core/project].
```

Replace PROJECT_ID with our project ID.

Setting a default compute zone

To set a default compute zone, run the following command:

```
gcloud config set compute/zone COMPUTE_ZONE
```

where COMPUTE_ZONE is the desired geographical compute zone, such as us-east4-a.

```
user@cloudshell:~ (kubernetesquickstart)$ gcloud config set compute/zone us-east4-a
Updated property [compute/zone].
```

Creating a Kubernetes Engine cluster

A cluster consists of at least one cluster master machine and multiple worker machines called nodes. Nodes are Compute Engine virtual machine (VM) instances that run the Kubernetes processes necessary to make them part of the cluster. We deploy applications to clusters, and the applications run on the nodes.

To create a cluster, run the following command:

```
gcloud container clusters create CLUSTER_NAME
```

where CLUSTER_NAME is the name we choose for the cluster.

```
user@cloudshell:~ (kubernetesquickstart)$ gcloud container clusters create kube-
quickstart-cluster

WARNING: Starting in 1.12, new clusters will have basic authentication disabled by
default. Basic authentication can be enabled (or disabled) manually using the `--[

no-]enable-basic-auth` flag.

WARNING: Starting in 1.12, new clusters will not have a client certificate issued. You
can manually enable (or disable) the issuance of the client certificate using

the `--[no-]issue-client-certificate` flag.

WARNING: Currently VPC-native is not the default mode during cluster creation. In the
future, this will become the default mode and can be disabled using `--no-enabl

e-ip-alias` flag. Use `--[no-]enable-ip-alias` flag to suppress this warning.

This will enable the autorepair feature for nodes. Please see

https://cloud.google.com/kubernetes-engine/docs/node-auto-repair for more

information on node autorepairs.

WARNING: Starting in Kubernetes v1.10, new clusters will no longer get compute-rw and
storage-ro scopes added to what is specified in --scopes (though the latter wil

l remain included in the default --scopes). To use these scopes, add them explicitly
to --scopes. To use the new behavior, set container/new_scopes_behavior property

 (gcloud config set container/new_scopes_behavior true).

Creating cluster kube-quickstart-cluster...done.

Created [https://container.googleapis.com/v1/projects/kubernetesquickstart/zones/us-
east4-a/clusters/kube-quickstart-cluster].

To inspect the contents of your cluster, go to:
https://console.cloud.google.com/kubernetes/workload_/gcloud/us-east4-a/kube-
quickstart-cluster?project=kubernetesqui

ckstart

kubeconfig entry generated for kube-quickstart-cluster.

NAME                    LOCATION     MASTER_VERSION  MASTER_IP     MACHINE_TYPE
NODE_VERSION  NUM_NODES  STATUS
```

Get authentication credentials for the cluster

After creating our cluster, we need to get authentication credentials to interact
with the cluster.

To authenticate for the cluster, run the following command:

```
 gcloud container clusters get-credentials CLUSTER_NAME
```

```
user@cloudshell:~ (kubernetesquickstart)$ gcloud container clusters get-credentials kube-quickstart-cluster
Fetching cluster endpoint and auth data.
kubeconfig entry generated for kube-quickstart-cluster.
```

This command configures kubectl to use the cluster we created.

Deploying an application to the cluster

Now that we have created a cluster, we can deploy a containerized application to it. For this quickstart, we can deploy our example web application, hello-app.

Kubernetes Engine uses Kubernetes objects to create and manage our cluster's resources. Kubernetes provides the Deployment object for deploying stateless applications like web servers. Service objects define rules and load balancing for accessing your application from the Internet.

To run hello-app in our cluster, run the following command:

```
kubectl run hello-server --image gcr.io/google-samples/hello-app:1.0 --port
8080

user@cloudshell:~ (kubernetesquickstart)$ kubectl run hello-server --image
gcr.io/google-samples/hello-app:1.0 --port 8080

deployment "hello-server" created
```

This Kubernetes command, kubectl run, creates a new Deployment named hello-server. The Deployment's Pod runs the hello-app image in its container.

In this command:

1. --image specifies a container image to deploy. In this case, the command pulls the example image from a Google Container Registry bucket, gcr.io/google-samples/hello-app. :1.0 indicates the specific image version to pull. If a version is not specified, the latest version is used.
2. --port specifies the port that the container exposes.

Exposing the Deployment

After deploying the application, we need to expose it to the Internet so that users can access it. We can expose our application by creating a Service, a Kubernetes resource that exposes our application to external traffic.

To expose our application, run the following kubectl expose command:

```
kubectl expose deployment hello-server --type LoadBalancer \
  --port 80 --target-port 8080
```

```
user@cloudshell:~ (kubernetesquickstart)$ kubectl expose deployment
hello-server --type LoadBalancer \
>    --port 80 --target-port 8080
service "hello-server" exposed
```

Passing in the --type LoadBalancer flag creates a Compute Engine load balancer for our container. The --port flag initializes public port 80 to the Internet and --target-port routes the traffic to port 8080 of the application.

Load balancers are billed per Compute Engine's load balancer pricing.

Inspecting and viewing the application

1. Inspect the hello-server Service by running kubectl get:

```
kubectl get service hello-server
user@cloudshell:~ (kubernetesquickstart)$ kubectl get service hello-server
NAME           TYPE            CLUSTER-IP      EXTERNAL-IP       PORT(S)        AGE
hello-server   LoadBalancer    10.55.253.77    35.186.182.150    80:30397/TCP   3m
```

From this command's output, copy the Service's external IP address from the EXTERNAL-IP column.

Note: We might need to wait several minutes before the Service's external IP address populates. If the application's external IP is <pending>, run kubectl get again.

2. View the application from our web browser using the external IP address with the exposed port:

```
http://EXTERNAL_IP/
```

We have just deployed a containerized web application to Kubernetes Engine!

Clean up

To avoid incurring charges to your Google Cloud Platform account for the resources used in this quickstart:

1. Delete the application's Service by running kubectl delete:

```
kubectl delete service hello-server
```

This will delete the Compute Engine load balancer that we created when we exposed the deployment.

```
user@cloudshell:~ (kubernetesquickstart)$ kubectl delete service hello-server
service "hello-server" deleted
```

Delete our cluster by running gcloud container clusters delete:

```
gcloud container clusters delete CLUSTER_NAME
user@cloudshell:~ (kubernetesquickstart)$ gcloud container clusters delete kube-quickstart-cluster
The following clusters will be deleted.
 - [kube-quickstart-cluster] in [us-east4-a]
Do you want to continue (Y/n)?  Y
Deleting cluster kube-quickstart-cluster...done.
Deleted [https://container.googleapis.com/v1/projects/kubernetesquickstart/zones/us-east4-a/clusters/kube-quickstart-cluster].
```

hello-app code

hello-app is a simple web server application consisting of two files: main.go and a Dockerfile.

hello-app is packaged as Docker container image. Container images are stored in any Docker image registry, such as Google Container Registry. We host hello-app in a Container Registry bucket named gcr.io/google-samples/hello-app.

hello-app/main.go:

```go
package main

import (
        "fmt"
        "log"
        "net/http"
        "os"
)


func main() {
        // use PORT environment variable, or default to 8080
        port := "8080"
        if fromEnv := os.Getenv("PORT"); fromEnv != "" {
                port = fromEnv
        }

        // register hello function to handle all requests
        server := http.NewServeMux()
        server.HandleFunc("/", hello)

        // start the web server on port and accept requests
        log.Printf("Server listening on port %s", port)
        err := http.ListenAndServe(":"+port, server)
        log.Fatal(err)
}


// hello responds to the request with a plain-text "Hello, world" message.
func hello(w http.ResponseWriter, r *http.Request) {
        log.Printf("Serving request: %s", r.URL.Path)
        host, _ := os.Hostname()
        fmt.Fprintf(w, "Hello, world!\n")
        fmt.Fprintf(w, "Version: 1.0.0\n")
        fmt.Fprintf(w, "Hostname: %s\n", host)
}
```

hello-app/Dockerfile:

```
FROM golang:1.8-alpine
ADD . /go/src/hello-app
RUN go install hello-app
FROM alpine:latest
COPY --from=0 /go/bin/hello-app
ENV PORT 8080
CMD ["./hello-app"]
```

CHAPTER 6: DEPLOYING A CONTAINERIZED WEB APPLICATION VIA KUBERNETES

Deploying a containerized web application

We'll learn how to package a web application in a Docker container image, and run that container image on a Kubernetes Engine cluster as a load-balanced set of replicas that can scale to the needs of your users.

To package and deploy our application on Kubernetes Engine, we need to do the followings:

1. Package the app into a Docker image
2. Run the container locally on the machine (optional)
3. Upload the image to a registry
4. Create a container cluster
5. Deploy the app to the cluster
6. Expose the app to the Internet
7. Scale up the deployment
8. Deploy a new version of the app

Prerequisites

Take the following steps to enable the Kubernetes Engine API as we've done in GCP: Kubernetes Quickstart:
Visit the Kubernetes Engine page in the Google Cloud Platform Console.
Create or select a project.
Wait for the API and related services to be enabled. This can take several minutes.

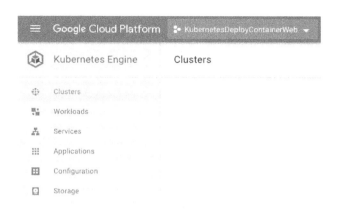

Using Google Cloud Shell

We'll use Google Cloud Shell, which comes preinstalled with the gcloud, docker, and kubectl command-line tools used in this tutorial. If we use Cloud Shell, we don't need to install these command-line tools on our local machine.

To use Google Cloud Shell:
Go to the Google Cloud Platform Console.
Click the Activate Cloud Shell button at the top of the console window.
A Cloud Shell session opens inside a new frame at the bottom of the console and displays a command-line prompt.

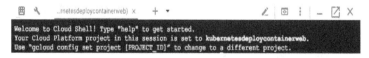

Set defaults for the gcloud command-line tool

We may want to set the defaults so that we can save time when we use command-line tool:

```
gcloud config set project PROJECT_ID
gcloud config set compute/zone ZONE
kihyuck_hong@cloudshell:~ (kubernetesdeploycontainerweb)$ gcloud
config set project kubernetesdeploycontainerweb

Updated property [core/project].|

kihyuck_hong@cloudshell:~ (kubernetesdeploycontainerweb)$ gcloud
config set compute/zone us-east4-a

Updated property [compute/zone].
```

Step 1: Build the container image

Kubernetes Engine accepts Docker images as the application deployment format. To build a Docker image, we need to have an application and a Dockerfile.

For this tutorial, we will deploy a sample web application called hello-app, a web server written in Go that responds to all requests with the message "Hello, World!" on port 80.

The application is packaged as a Docker image, using the Dockerfile that contains instructions on how the image is built. We will use this file to package the application below.

To download the hello-app source code, run the following commands:

```
user@cloudshell:~ (kubernetesdeploycontainerweb)$ git clone
https://github.com/GoogleCloudPlatform/kubernetes-engine-samples

user@cloudshell:~ (kubernetesdeploycontainerweb)$ cd kubernetes-
engine-samples/hello-app

user@cloudshell:~/kubernetes-engine-samples/hello-app
(kubernetesdeploycontainerweb)$
```

Set the PROJECT_ID environment variable in our shell by retrieving the pre-configured project ID on gcloud by running the command below:

```
user@cloudshell:~/kubernetes-engine-samples/hello-app (kubernetesdeploycontainerweb)$
export PROJECT_ID="$(gcloud config get-value project -q)"|

Your active configuration is: [cloudshell-19280]
```

The value of PROJECT_ID will be used to tag the container image for pushing it to our private Container Registry.

To build the container image of this application and tag it for uploading, run the following command:

```
user@cloudshell:~/kubernetes-engine-samples/hello-app
(kubernetesdeploycontainerweb)$ docker build -t gcr.io/${PROJECT_ID}/hello-
app:v1 .

...

Successfully built 15f56228a80e|

Successfully tagged gcr.io/kubernetesdeploycontainerweb/hello-app:v1
```

This command instructs Docker to build the image using the Dockerfile in the current directory:

```
user@cloudshell:~/kubernetes-engine-samples/hello-app
(kubernetesdeploycontainerweb)$ ls

Dockerfile  main.go  manifests  README.md
```

and tag it with a name, such as gcr.io/my-project/hello-app:v1. The gcr.io prefix refers to Google Container Registry, where the image will be hosted. Running this command does not upload the image yet.

We can run docker images command to verify that the build was successful:

```
user@cloudshell:~/kubernetes-engine-samples/hello-app
(kubernetesdeploycontainerweb)$ docker images|
```

Output:

```
REPOSITORY                                        TAG IMAGE ID       CREATED       SIZE
gcr.io/kubernetesdeploycontainerweb/hello-app  v1  15f56228a80e  3 minutes ago  10.3MB
```

Step 2: Upload the container image

Now, we need to upload the container image to a registry so that Kubernetes Engine can download and run it.

First, configure Docker command-line tool to authenticate to Container Registry (we need to run this only once):

```
user@cloudshell:~/kubernetes-engine-samples/hello-app (kubernetesdeploycontainerweb)$ gcloud auth
configure-docker

WARNING: Your config file at [/home/user/.docker/config.json] contains these credential helper
entries:

...

Docker configuration file updated.
```

We can now use the Docker command-line tool to upload the image to our Container Registry:

```
user@cloudshell:~/kubernetes-engine-samples/hello-app
(kubernetesdeploycontainerweb)$ docker push gcr.io/${PROJECT_ID}/hello-app:v1

The push refers to repository [gcr.io/kubernetesdeploycontainerweb/hello-app]

ed7a2efbc124: Pushed
```

Step 3: Run our container locally (optional)

To test our container image using our local Docker engine, run the following command:

```
user@cloudshell:~/kubernetes-engine-samples/hello-app (kubernetesdeploycontainerweb)$
docker run --rm -p 8080:8080 gcr.io/${PROJECT_ID}/hello-app:v1

2018/09/12 21:19:31 Server listening on port 8080
```

If we're on Cloud Shell, we can can click "Web preview" button on the top right to see our application running in a browser tab.

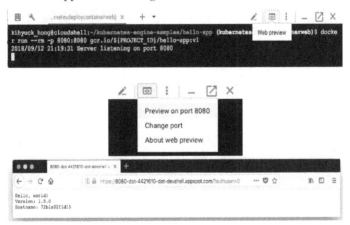

Otherwise, open a new terminal window (or a Cloud Shell tab) and run to verify if the container works and responds to requests with "Hello, World!":

```
user@cloudshell:~ (kubernetesdeploycontainerweb)$ curl http://localhost:8080
Hello, world!
Version: 1.0.0|
Hostname: 72b1a02f1d15
```

Once we've seen a successful response, we can shut down the container by pressing Ctrl+C in the tab where docker run command is running.

Step 4: Create a container cluster

Now that the container image is stored in a registry, we need to create a container cluster to run the container image.
First, we may try to use console to create the cluster.

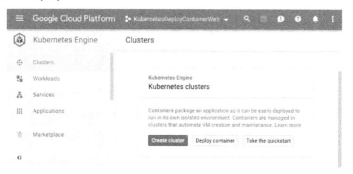

A cluster consists of a pool of Compute Engine VM instances running Kubernetes, the open source cluster orchestration system that powers Kubernetes Engine.

Once we have created a Kubernetes Engine cluster, we use Kubernetes to deploy applications to the cluster and manage the applications' lifecycle.

We've already create the cluster via console, however, we will run the following command to create a two-node cluster named bogo-hello-cluster via command-line:
It may take several minutes for the cluster to be created.

```
user@cloudshell:~/kubernetes-engine-samples/hello-app (kubernetesdeploycontainerweb)$
gcloud container clusters create bogo-hello-cluster --num-nodes=

2 --zone=us-east4-a

...

kubeconfig entry generated for bogo-hello-cluster.
NAME                 LOCATION     MASTER_VERSION  MASTER_IP      MACHINE_TYPE
NODE_VERSION  NUM_NODES  STATUS

bogo-hello-cluster  us-east4-a  1.9.7-gke.6      35.236.195.6  n1-standard-1  1.9.7-
gke.6    2          RUNNING
```

Once the command has completed, run the following command and see the cluster's three worker VM instances:

```
user@cloudshell:~/kubernetes-engine-samples/hello-app (kubernetesdeploycontainerweb)$ gcloud compute instances list
NAME                                                     ZONE         MACHINE_TYPE   PREEMPTIBLE  INTERNAL_IP  EXTERNAL_IP    STATUS
gke-bogo-hello-cluster-default-pool-0e1d32c3-4cml  us-east4-a  n1-standard-1                  10.150.0.6   35.221.25.147  RUNNING
gke-bogo-hello-cluster-default-pool-0e1d32c3-mxqw  us-east4-a  n1-standard-1                  10.150.0.5   35.221.18.79   RUNNING
```

Note: If we are using an existing Kubernetes Engine cluster or if we have created a cluster through Google Cloud Platform Console, we need to run the following command to retrieve cluster credentials and configure kubectl command-line tool with them:

```
$ gcloud container clusters get-credentials bogo-hello-cluster
```

If we have already created a cluster with the gcloud container clusters create command listed above, this step is not necessary.

Step 5: Deploy the application

To deploy and manage applications on a Kubernetes Engine cluster, we must communicate with the Kubernetes cluster management system. We typically do this by using the kubectl command-line tool.

Kubernetes represents applications as Pods, which are units that represent a container (or group of tightly-coupled containers). The Pod is the smallest deployable unit in Kubernetes.

In this tutorial, each Pod contains only our hello-app container.

The kubectl run command below causes Kubernetes to create a Deployment named hello-web on our cluster. The Deployment manages multiple copies of our application, called replicas, and schedules them to run on the individual nodes in our cluster. In this case, the Deployment will be running only one Pod of our application.

Run the following command to deploy our application, listening on port 8080:

```
user@cloudshell:~/kubernetes-engine-samples/hello-app (kubernetesdeploycontainerweb)$
kubectl run hello-web --image=gcr.io/${PROJECT_ID}/hello-app:v1

--port 8080

deployment "hello-web" created
```

To see the Pod created by the Deployment, run the following command:

```
user@cloudshell:~/kubernetes-engine-samples/hello-app (kubernetesdeploycontainerweb)$ kubectl get pods

NAME                            READY    STATUS     RESTARTS    AGE
hello-web-85455bbc49-xkbqp      1/1      Running    0           44m
```

Step 6: Expose the application to the Internet

By default, the containers we run on Kubernetes Engine are not accessible from the Internet, because they do not have external IP addresses. We must explicitly expose our application to traffic from the Internet, run the following command:

```
$ kubectl expose deployment hello-web --type=LoadBalancer --port 80 --target-port 8080

service "hello-web" exposed
```

The kubectl expose command above creates a Service resource, which provides networking and IP support to our application's Pods. Kubernetes Engine creates an external IP and a Load Balancer (subject to billing) for our application.

The --port flag specifies the port number configured on the Load Balancer, and the --target-port flag specifies the port number that is used by the Pod created by the kubectl run command from the previous step.

Note: Kubernetes Engine assigns the external IP address to the Service resource—not the Deployment. If we want to find out the external IP that Kubernetes Engine provisioned for our application, we can inspect the Service with the kubectl get service command:

```
user@cloudshell:~ (kubernetesdeploycontainerweb)$ kubectl get service
NAME         TYPE          CLUSTER-IP      EXTERNAL-IP     PORT(S)        AGE
hello-web    LoadBalancer  10.59.247.225   35.188.240.248  80:30420/TCP   8m
```

Once we've determined the external IP address for our application, copy the IP address. Point our browser to this URL (such as http://35.188.240.248) to check if our application is accessible.

Step 7: Scale up the application

We add more replicas to our application's Deployment resource by using the kubectl scale command. To add two additional replicas to our Deployment (for a total of three), run the following command:

```
user@cloudshell:~ (kubernetesdeploycontainerweb)$ kubectl scale deployment hello-web --replicas=3
deployment "hello-web" scaled
```

We can see the new replicas running on our cluster by running the following commands:

```
user@cloudshell:~ (kubernetesdeploycontainerweb)$ kubectl get deployment hello-web
NAME         DESIRED   CURRENT   UP-TO-DATE   AVAILABLE   AGE
hello-web    3         3         3            3           2h
user@cloudshell:~ (kubernetesdeploycontainerweb)$ kubectl get pods
NAME                          READY   STATUS    RESTARTS   AGE
hello-web-85455bbc49-4xggn    1/1     Running   0          2m
hello-web-85455bbc49-hdcxr    1/1     Running   0          2m
hello-web-85455bbc49-xkbqp    1/1     Running   0          2h
```

Now, we have multiple instances of our application running independently of each other and we can use the kubectl scale command to adjust capacity of our application.
The load balancer we provisioned in the previous step will start routing traffic to these new replicas automatically.

Step 8: Deploy a new version of the app

Kubernetes Engine's rolling update mechanism ensures that our application remains up and available even as the system replaces instances of our old container image with our new one across all the running replicas.

We can create an image for the v2 version of our application by building the same source code and tagging it as v2 (or we can change the "Hello, World!" string to "Hello, Kubernetes Engine!" before building the image):

```
user@cloudshell:~/kubernetes-engine-samples/hello-app (kubernetesdeploycontainerweb)$ pwd

/home/user/kubernetes-engine-samples/hello-app

user@cloudshell:~/kubernetes-engine-samples/hello-app (kubernetesdeploycontainerweb)$ ls

Dockerfile  main.go  manifests  README.md

user@cloudshell:~/kubernetes-engine-samples/hello-app (kubernetesdeploycontainerweb)$ docker
build -t gcr.io/${PROJECT_ID}/hello-app:v2 .

...

Successfully built f50f178f02e2

Successfully tagged gcr.io/kubernetesdeploycontainerweb/hello-app:v2
```

Then push the image to the Google Container Registry:

```
user@cloudshell:~/kubernetes-engine-samples/hello-app
(kubernetesdeploycontainerweb)$ gcloud docker -- push
gcr.io/${PROJECT_ID}/hello-app:v2
```

Now, apply a rolling update to the existing deployment with an image update:

```
user@cloudshell:~/kubernetes-engine-samples/hello-app (kubernetesdeploycontainerweb)$
kubectl set image deployment/hello-web hello-web=gcr.io/${PROJEC

T_ID}/hello-app:v2

deployment "hello-web" image updated
```

Visit our application again at http://[EXTERNAL_IP], and observe the changes we made take effect.

```
user@cloudshell:~/kubernetes-engine-samples/hello-app (kubernetesdeploycontainerweb)$ kubectl get service

NAME       TYPE          CLUSTER-IP     EXTERNAL-IP      PORT(S)       AGE

hello-web  LoadBalancer  10.59.247.225  35.188.240.248   80:30420/TCP  1h
```

Cleaning up

To avoid incurring charges to our Google Cloud Platform account for the resources used in this tutorial.

After completing this tutorial, follow these steps to remove the following resources to prevent unwanted charges incurring on our account:

Delete the Service: This step will deallocate the Cloud Load Balancer created for our Service:

```
user@cloudshell:~/kubernetes-engine-samples/hello-app
(kubernetesdeploycontainerweb)$ kubectl delete service hello-web
```

service "hello-web" deleted

Wait for the Load Balancer provisioned for the hello-web Service to be deleted: The load balancer is deleted asynchronously in the background when you run kubectl delete. Wait until the load balancer is deleted by watching the output of the following command:

```
user@cloudshell:~/kubernetes-engine-samples/hello-app
(kubernetesdeploycontainerweb)$ gcloud compute forwarding-rules list

Listed 0 items.
```

Delete the container cluster: This step will delete the resources that make up the container cluster, such as the compute instances, disks and network resources.

```
user@cloudshell:~/kubernetes-engine-samples/hello-app (kubernetesdeploycontainerweb)$
gcloud container clusters delete bogo-hello-cluster

The following clusters will be deleted.

 - [bogo-hello-cluster] in [us-east4-a]

Do you want to continue (Y/n)?  Y

Deleting cluster bogo-hello-cluster...done.

Deleted
[https://container.googleapis.com/v1/projects/kubernetesdeploycontainerweb/zones/us-
east4-a/clusters/bogo-hello-cluster].
```

CHAPTER 7: DJANGO DEPLOY VIA KUBERNETES I (LOCAL)

Note

In this tutorial, we'll use two dev machines for a local test before we deploying the app to Kubernetes:
local - GCP console
local - my MacBook Air

Django tutorial app

We'll deploy the official Django tutorial app to Google Kubernetes Engine. The app's models represent polls that contain questions, and we can interact with the models using the Django admin console.

Getting Started With Django

There are four main options (Getting Started With Django) for deploying Django on Cloud Platform.

Django Deployment Option	Use if you want	Don't use if you need	Get Started
GOOGLE APP ENGINE STANDARD ENVIRONMENT	• Minimal configuration • No server maintenance • Easy scalability	• System libraries not available in the App Engine standard Python environment	DJANGO ON APP ENGINE STANDARD ENVIRONMENT
GOOGLE APP ENGINE FLEXIBLE ENVIRONMENT	• Most of the advantages of App Engine • System libraries and Python libraries that depend on them • Custom Docker runtimes	• Control over the entire VM (outside of the application's docker container)	DJANGO ON APP ENGINE FLEXIBLE ENVIRONMENT
GOOGLE KUBERNETES ENGINE	• Django containers in a microservice environment • A toolkit to design your own container-based platform	• A fully-featured platform as a service. For a container-based PaaS, consider flexible environment.	DJANGO ON KUBERNETES ENGINE
GOOGLE COMPUTE ENGINE	• Familiar infrastructure as a service using VMs • Windows VMs	• A serverless environment without the need to configure your own infrastructure	DJANGO IN GOOGLE CLOUD PLATFORM MARKETPLACE

The Django object-relational mapper (ORM) works best with a traditional SQL database. If we are starting a new project, Google Cloud SQL is a good choice.

App Engine comes with a built-in Memcached service.

To install Memcached on Compute Engine, we can use GCP Marketplace. To install Memcached on either Compute Engine or Kubernetes Engine, we can use the Memcached Docker image.

Similarly we can install Redis by using GCP Marketplace or the Redis docker image.

For task queuing, App Engine comes with a built-in task queue feature for long-running background jobs. Outside of App Engine, consider the massively scalable Cloud Pub/Sub service, which can be turned into a task queue using Cloud Pub/Sub Task Queue for Python (psq).

Other popular task queuing options, available in GCP Marketplace, include RabbitMQ and Kafka. There are also Docker images for RabbitMQ and Kafka.

Prerequisites

Before we begin, here are the check list we need complete it.

1. Create a project in the Google Cloud Platform Console.

If haven't already created a project, create one now. Projects enable us to manage all Google Cloud Platform resources for our app, including deployment, access control, billing, and services.

    a)   Open the GCP Console.
    b)   In the drop-down menu at the top, select Create a project.
    c)   Give the project a name.
    d)   Make a note of the project ID, which might be different from the project name. The project ID is used in commands and in configurations.

New Project

Project Name *
Django-Poll-App

Project ID: django-poll-app-216501. It cannot be changed later.   EDIT

Location *
No organization   BROWSE
Parent organization or folder

CREATE   CANCEL

2. Install the Google Cloud SDK.

If haven't already installed the Google Cloud SDK, install and initialize the Google Cloud SDK now. The SDK contains tools and libraries that enable us to create and manage resources on Google Cloud Platform.

3. Enable APIs for our project.

This takes us to the GCP Console and automatically enables the APIs used by this tutorial. The APIs used are: Cloud SQL API, Compute Engine API.

Cloning the Django app (Cloud Shell)

The code for the Django sample app is in the Google Cloud Platform repository on GitHub.
Clone the repository to our local machine:

```
user@cloudshell:~ (django-poll-app-216501)$ git clone
https://github.com/GoogleCloudPlatform/python-docs-samples.git
```

Go to the directory that contains the sample code:

```
user@cloudshell:~ (django-poll-app-216501)$ cd python-docs-
samples/container_engine/django_tutorial

user@cloudshell:~/python-docs-samples/container_engine/django_tutorial (django-poll-
app-216501)$|
```

Alternatively, we can download the sample as a zip and extract it.

Setting up local environment (Cloud Shell)

When deployed, our application uses the Cloud SQL Proxy that is built in to the App Engine environment to communicate with our Cloud SQL instance.
The Cloud SQL Proxy works by having a local client, called the proxy, running in the local environment. Our application communicates with the proxy with the standard database protocol used by our database. The proxy uses a secure tunnel to communicate with its companion process running on the server.

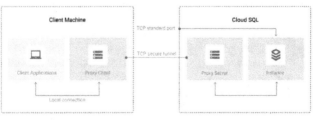

However, to test our application locally, we must install and use a local copy of the Cloud SQL Proxy in our development environment.

To perform basic administrative tasks on our Cloud SQL instance, we can use the PostgreSQL Client.

Note: We must authenticate gcloud to use the proxy to connect from our local machine.

Install the SQL proxy (Cloud Shell)

Download and install the Cloud SQL Proxy. The Cloud SQL Proxy is used to connect to our Cloud SQL instance when running locally.

We can install the proxy anywhere in your local environment. The location of the proxy binaries does not impact where it listens for data from your application.

For Linux 64-BIT:

Download the proxy:

```
wget https://dl.google.com/cloudsql/cloud_sql_proxy.linux.amd64 -O cloud_sql_proxy

user@cloudshell:~/python-docs-samples/container_engine/django_tutorial (django-poll-app-216501)$ wget https://dl.google.com/cloudsql/cloud_sql_proxy.linux

.amd64 -O cloud_sql_proxy
```

Make the proxy executable:

```
$ chmod +x cloud_sql_proxy

user@cloudshell:~/python-docs-samples/container_engine/django_tutorial (django-poll-app-216501)$
chmod +x cloud_sql_proxy

$ ls -l

total 7308

-rw-r--r-- 1 user user        0 Sep 14 21:55 ]

-rwxr-xr-x 1 user user 7448368 Sep 14 22:00 cloud_sql_proxy

-rw-r--r-- 1 user user     1241 Sep 14 21:48 Dockerfile

-rw-r--r-- 1 user user        0 Sep 14 21:48 __init__.py

-rw-r--r-- 1 user user      881 Sep 14 21:48 Makefile

-rwxr-xr-x 1 user user      825 Sep 14 21:48 manage.py

drwxr-xr-x 2 user user     4096 Sep 14 21:48 mysite

drwxr-xr-x 3 user user     4096 Sep 14 21:48 polls

-rw-r--r-- 1 user user     3591 Sep 14 21:48 polls.yaml

-rw-r--r-- 1 user user     1161 Sep 14 21:48 README.md

-rw-r--r-- 1 user user       79 Sep 14 21:48 requirements.txt
```

Create a Cloud SQL instance

1. **Create a Cloud SQL for PostgreSQL instance.**

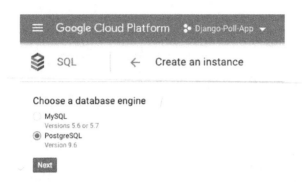

Name the instance as polls-instance. It can take a few minutes for the instance to be ready. After the instance is ready, it should be visible in the instances list.

Now use the Cloud SDK from command line to run the following command. Copy the value shown for connectionName for the next step.

```
gcloud sql instances describe [INSTANCE_NAME]

user@cloudshell:~/python-docs-samples/container_engine/django_tutorial (django-poll-app-216501)$
gcloud sql instances describe polls-instance

backendType: SECOND_GEN

connectionName: django-poll-app-216501:us-east4:polls-instance

databaseVersion: POSTGRES_9_6

etag: '"v2uwXMbh3d1V5GKTL9aEU1EZQxc/MQ"'

gceZone: us-east4-c

instanceType: CLOUD_SQL_INSTANCE

ipAddresses:

- ipAddress: 35.236.201.91
```

The connectionName value is in the format [PROJECT_NAME]:[REGION_NAME]:[INSTANCE_NAME].

Initialize the Cloud SQL instance (Cloud Shell)

Start the Cloud SQL Proxy using the connectionName from the previous step. Linux/Mac OS X

```
./cloud_sql_proxy -instances="[INSTANCE_CONNECTION_NAME]"=tcp:5432
```

Replace [INSTANCE_CONNECTION_NAME] with the value of connectionName that we recorded in the previous step.

```
user@cloudshell:~/python-docs-samples/container_engine/django_tutorial (django-poll-app-216501)$
./cloud_sql_proxy -instances="django-poll-app-216501:us-east4:polls-instance"=tcp:5432

2018/09/14 22:55:26 Listening on 127.0.0.1:5432 for django-poll-app-216501:us-east4:polls-instance

2018/09/14 22:55:26 Ready for new connections
```

This step establishes a connection from our local computer (in this case, Cloud Shell) to our Cloud SQL instance for local testing purposes. Keep the Cloud SQL Proxy running the entire time we test our application locally.

First GCP shell:

```
kihyuck_hong@cloudshell:~/python-docs-samples/container_engine/django_tutorial (django-poll-app-216501)
$ ./cloud_sql_proxy -instances="django-poll-app-216501:us-east4:polls-instance"=tcp:5432
2018/09/14 22:55:26 Listening on 127.0.0.1:5432 for django-poll-app-216501:us-east4:polls-instance
2018/09/14 22:55:26 Ready for new connections
```

The 2nd shell (new):

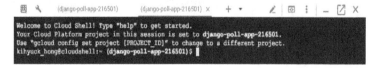

```
Welcome to Cloud Shell! Type "help" to get started.
Your Cloud Platform project in this session is set to django-poll-app-216501.
Use "gcloud config set project [PROJECT_ID]" to change to a different project.
kihyuck_hong@cloudshell:~ (django-poll-app-216501)$
```

Create a new Cloud SQL user and database (Cloud Shell)

On a Postgres client:
In a separate command-line tab, install the Postgres client.

```
sudo apt-get install postgresql
user@cloudshell:~ (django-poll-app-216501)$ sudo apt-get install postgresql
```

Use the Postgres client or similar program to connect to our instance. When prompted, use the root password we configured.

```
psql --host 127.0.0.1 --user postgres -password
user@cloudshell:~ (django-poll-app-216501)$ psql --host 127.0.0.1 --user postgres --password
Password for user postgres:
psql (9.6.10, server 9.6.6)
Type "help" for help.|
postgres=>
```

Create the required databases, users, and access permissions in our Cloud SQL database using the commands below. Replace [POSTGRES_USER] and [POSTGRES_PASSWORD] with the desired username and password.

```
CREATE DATABASE polls;|
CREATE USER [POSTGRES_USER] WITH PASSWORD '[POSTGRES_PASSWORD]';
GRANT ALL PRIVILEGES ON DATABASE polls TO [POSTGRES_USER];
GRANT ALL PRIVILEGES ON ALL TABLES IN SCHEMA public TO [POSTGRES_USER];
postgres=> CREATE DATABASE polls;
CREATE DATABASE
postgres=> CREATE USER khong WITH PASSWORD 'postgres';
CREATE ROLE
postgres=> GRANT ALL PRIVILEGES ON DATABASE polls TO khong;
GRANT
postgres=> GRANT ALL PRIVILEGES ON ALL TABLES IN SCHEMA public TO khong;
GRANT
postgres=>
```

Creating a service account

The proxy requires a service account with Editor privileges for our Cloud SQL instance.

Note: To create a service account with the required permissions, the user we are logged in as must have the resourcemanager.projects.setIamPolicy permission. This permission is included in the Project Owner role, as well as the Project IAM Admin and Organization Administrator roles.

We must also have enabled the Cloud SQL Admin API.

1. Go to the Cloud SQL Service accounts page of the Google Cloud Platform Console.
2. If needed, select the project that contains our Cloud SQL instance.

3. Click Creare service account
4. In the Create service account dialog, provide a descriptive name for the service account.

5. For Role, select one of the following roles:

    a. Cloud SQL > Cloud SQL Client
    b. Cloud SQL > Cloud SQL Editor
    c. Cloud SQL > Cloud SQL Admin

Create service account

A service account represents a Google Cloud service identity, such as code running on Compute Engine VMS, App Engine apps, or systems running outside Google.

Service account name

CloudSQL-Service-Account

Display name for this service account

Service account ID

cloudsql-service-account   @django-poll-app-216501.iam.gservice ✕ C

Project role ❓

Role

Cloud SQL Admin   ▼   🗑

Full control of Cloud SQL resources.

Role

Cloud SQL Editor   ▼   🗑

Full control of existing Cloud SQL instances excluding modifying users, SSL certificates or deleting resources.

Role

Cloud SQL Client   ▼   🗑

Connectivity access to Cloud SQL instances.

+ ADD ANOTHER ROLE

6. Change the Service account ID to a unique value that we will recognize so we can easily find this service account later if needed.
7. Click Furnish a new private key.
8. The default key type is JSON, which is the correct value to use.

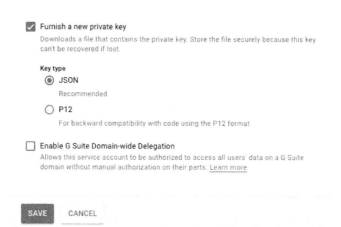

✓ **Furnish a new private key**
Downloads a file that contains the private key. Store the file securely because this key can't be recovered if lost.

Key type
◉ JSON
    Recommended

○ P12
    For backward compatibility with code using the P12 format

☐ **Enable G Suite Domain-wide Delegation**
Allows this service account to be authorized to access all users' data on a G Suite domain without manual authorization on their parts. Learn more

SAVE   CANCEL

9. Click Create.

Service account and key created

Service account CloudSQL-Service-Account created. The account's private key django-poll-app-216501-f4ffa0d2f930.json saved on your computer.

⚠ django-poll-app-216501-f4ffa0d2f930.json allows access to your cloud resources, so store it securely. Learn more

The private key file is downloaded to our machine. We can move it to another location. Keep the key file secure.

Service accounts   + CREATE SERVICE ACCOUNT   🗑 DELETE

Service accounts for project "Django-Poll-App"

A service account represents a Google Cloud service identity, such as code running on Compute Engine VMs, App Engine apps, or systems running outside Google. Learn more

	Email	Name ↑	Key ID
☐	🔑 cloudsql-service-account@django-poll-app-216501.iam.gserviceaccount.com	CloudSQL-Service-Account	f4ffa0d2f93(
☐	🔑 798345995815-compute@developer.gserviceaccount.com	Compute Engine default service account	No keys

Configuring the database settings (Cloud Shell)

Now, we want to set environment variables for database access for local testing:

```
export DATABASE_USER=<your-database-user>
export DATABASE_PASSWORD=<your-database-password>
user@cloudshell:~ (django-poll-app-216501)$ export DATABASE_USER=khong
user@cloudshell:~ (django-poll-app-216501)$ export DATABASE_PASSWORD=postgres
```

Setting up our GKE configuration (Cloud Shell)

1. This application is represented in a single Kubernetes configuration, called polls. In polls.yaml replace <your-project-id> with our project ID.

```
kihyuck_hong@cloudshell:~/python-docs-samples/container_engine/django_tutorial
(django-poll-app-216501)$ ls -l
total 7364
-rw-r--r-- 1 kihyuck_hong kihyuck_hong       0 Sep 14 21:55 ]
-rwxr-xr-x 1 kihyuck_hong kihyuck_hong 7505002 Sep  7 17:31 cloud_sql_proxy
-rw-r--r-- 1 kihyuck_hong kihyuck_hong    1241 Sep 14 21:48 Dockerfile
-rw-r--r-- 1 kihyuck_hong kihyuck_hong       0 Sep 14 21:48 __init__.py
-rw-r--r-- 1 kihyuck_hong kihyuck_hong     881 Sep 14 21:48 Makefile
-rwxr-xr-x 1 kihyuck_hong kihyuck_hong     825 Sep 14 21:48 manage.py
drwxr-xr-x 2 kihyuck_hong kihyuck_hong    4096 Sep 14 21:48 mysite
drwxr-xr-x 3 kihyuck_hong kihyuck_hong    4096 Sep 14 21:48 polls
-rw-r--r-- 1 kihyuck_hong kihyuck_hong    3591 Sep 14 21:48 polls.yaml
-rw-r--r-- 1 kihyuck_hong kihyuck_hong    1161 Sep 14 21:48 README.md
-rw-r--r-- 1 kihyuck_hong kihyuck_hong      79 Sep 14 21:48 requirements.txt
```

2. In polls.yaml replace <your-cloudsql-connection-string> with the value of connectionName outputted from the following command:

```
gcloud beta sql instances describe [YOUR_INSTANCE_NAME]
user@cloudshell:~/python-docs-samples/container_engine/django_tutorial (django-poll-app-216501)$
gcloud beta sql instances describe polls-instance
backendType: SECOND_GEN
connectionName: django-poll-app-216501:us-east4:polls-instance
```

```
# [START proxy_container]
- image: b.gcr.io/cloudsql-docker/gce-proxy:1.05
  name: cloudsql-proxy
  command: ["/cloud_sql_proxy", "--dir=/cloudsql",
            "-instances=<your-cloudsql-connection-string>=tcp:5432",
            "-credential_file=/secrets/cloudsql/credentials.json"]
  volumeMounts:
    - name: cloudsql-oauth-credentials
      mountPath: /secrets/cloudsql
      readOnly: true
    - name: ssl-certs
      mountPath: /etc/ssl/certs
    - name: cloudsql
      mountPath: /cloudsql
# [START proxy_container]
- image: b.gcr.io/cloudsql-docker/gce-proxy:1.05
  name: cloudsql-proxy
  command: ["/cloud_sql_proxy", "--dir=/cloudsql",
            "-instances=django-poll-app-216501:us-east4:polls-instance=tcp:5432",
            "-credential_file=/secrets/cloudsql/credentials.json"]
  volumeMounts:
    - name: cloudsql-oauth-credentials
      mountPath: /secrets/cloudsql
      readOnly: true
    - name: ssl-certs
      mountPath: /etc/ssl/certs
    - name: cloudsql
      mountPath: /cloudsql
```

Running the app on our local computer (Cloud Shell)

1. To run the Django app on our local computer, we need to set up a Python development environment, including Python, pip, and virtualenv.
2. Create an isolated Python environment, and install dependencies:

```
virtualenv venv

source venv/bin/activate

pip install -r requirements.txt

user@cloudshell:~/python-docs-samples/container_engine/django_tutorial (django-poll-app-216501)$
virtualenv venv

Using base prefix '/usr'

New python executable in /home/user/python-docs-
samples/container_engine/django_tutorial/venv/bin/python3

Not overwriting existing python script l/home/user/python-docs-
samples/container_engine/django_tutorial/venv/bin/python (you must use /home/user/pyth

on-docs-samples/container_engine/django_tutorial/venv/bin/python3)

Installing setuptools, pip, wheel...done.

user@cloudshell:~/python-docs-samples/container_engine/django_tutorial (django-poll-app-216501)$
source venv/bin/activate

(venv) user@cloudshell:~/python-docs-samples/container_engine/django_tutorial (django-poll-app-
216501)$
```

But I got the following error "mysql_config not found":

```
(venv) user@cloudshell:~/python-docs-samples/container_engine/django_tutorial (django-poll-app-
216501)$ pip install -r requirements.txt

Collecting Django==2.1 (from -r requirements.txt (line 1))

  Using cached
https://files.pythonhosted.org/packages/51/1a/e0ac7886c7123a03814178d7517dc822af0fe51a72e1a6bff26
153103322/Django-2.1-py3-none-any.whl

Collecting mysqlclient==1.3.13 (from -r requirements.txt (line 2))

  Using cached
https://files.pythonhosted.org/packages/ec/fd/83329b9d3e14f7344d1cb31f128e6dbba70c5975c9e57896815
dbb1988ad/mysqlclient-1.3.13.tar.gz

    Complete output from command python setup.py egg_info:

    /bin/sh: 1: mysql_config: not found

    Traceback (most recent call last):

      File "", line 1, in

      File "/tmp/pip-install-fzfeevpd/mysqlclient/setup.py", line 18, in |

        metadata, options = get_config()

      File "/tmp/pip-install-fzfeevpd/mysqlclient/setup_posix.py", line 53, in get_config

        libs = mysql_config("libs_r")

      File "/tmp/pip-install-fzfeevpd/mysqlclient/setup_posix.py", line 28, in mysql_config

        raise EnvironmentError("%s not found" % (mysql_config.path,))

    OSError: mysql_config not found

    ----------------------------------------

Command "python setup.py egg_info" failed with error code 1 in /tmp/pip-install-
fzfeevpd/mysqlclient/
```

Installing "libmysqlclient-dev" resolved the issue:

```
user@cloudshell:/usr/local/bin (django-poll-app-216501)$ sudo apt-get install
libmysqlclient-dev
```

3. Run the Django migrations to set up our models:

```
python manage.py makemigrations
python manage.py makemigrations polls
python manage.py migrate
```

4. Start a local web server:

```
python manage.py runserver
```

5. Go to **http://localhost:8000**.

```
(venv) user@cloudshell:~/python-docs-samples/container_engine/django_tutorial
(django-poll-app-216501)
$ curl http://localhost
:8000
Hello, world. You're at the polls index.
```

We should see a simple webpage with the following text: "Hello, world. You're at the polls index." The sample app pages are delivered by the Django web server running on our computer. When we're ready to move forward, press Ctrl+C to stop the local web server.

Cloning the Django app (On Mac)

The code for the Django sample app is in the GCP Python Samples repository on GitHub.
Clone the repository to our local machine:

```
~/Documents/Django/Kubernetes$ git clone
https://github.com/GoogleCloudPlatform/python-docs-samples.git
```

Go to the directory that contains the sample code:

```
~/Documents/Django/Kubernetes$ cd python-docs-samples/container_engine/django_tutorial
Sam.ple-Air:django_tutorial sam.ple$
```

Alternatively, we can download the sample as a zip and extract it.

Setting up local environment (On Mac)

When deployed, our application uses the Cloud SQL Proxy that is built in to the App Engine environment to communicate with our Cloud SQL instance.

The Cloud SQL Proxy works by having a local client, called the proxy, running in the local environment. Our application communicates with the proxy with the standard database protocol used by our database. The proxy uses a secure tunnel to communicate with its companion process running on the server.

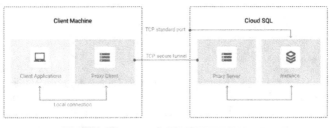

3rd Party Code Cloud SQL Code

However, to test our application locally, we must install and use a local copy of the Cloud SQL Proxy in our development environment.

To perform basic administrative tasks on our Cloud SQL instance, we can use the PostgreSQL Client.

Note: We must authenticate gcloud to use the proxy to connect from our local machine.

Install the SQL proxy (On Mac)

Download and install the Cloud SQL Proxy. The Cloud SQL Proxy is used to connect to our Cloud SQL instance when running locally.

We can install the proxy anywhere in your local environment. The location of the proxy binaries does not impact where it listens for data from your application.

For Mac 64-BIT:

1. Download the proxy:

```
curl -o cloud_sql_proxy https://dl.google.com/cloudsql/cloud_sql_proxy.darwin.386

Sam.ple-Air:Kubernetes sam.ple$ curl -o cloud_sql_proxy
https://dl.google.com/cloudsql/cloud_sql_proxy.darwin.386
```

2. Make the proxy executable:

```
$ chmod +x cloud_sql_proxy
```

Create a Cloud SQL instance (On Mac)

1. Create a Cloud SQL for PostgreSQL instance.

Not related to local environment. So, we don't need to do anymore. We can use the same Cloud SQL instance we setup in the earlier section (Cloud shell local).

2. We need to set a default project, run the following command from our local machine:

```
gcloud config set project PROJECT_ID
Sam.ple-Air:Kubernetes sam.ple$ $ gcloud config set project django-poll-app-216501
Updated property [core/project].
```

3. Now use the Cloud SDK from command line to run the following command. Copy the value shown for connectionName for the next step.

```
gcloud sql instances describe [INSTANCE_NAME]
Sam.ple-Air:Kubernetes sam.ple$ gcloud sql instances describe polls-instance
backendType: SECOND_GEN
connectionName: django-poll-app-216501:us-east4:polls-instance
databaseVersion: POSTGRES_9_6
etag: '"v2uwXMbh3dlV5GKTL9aEU1EZQxc/MQ"'
gceZone: us-east4-c
instanceType: CLOUD_SQL_INSTANCE
ipAddresses:
- ipAddress: 35.236.201.91
  type: PRIMARY
kind: sql#instance
name: polls-instance
project: django-poll-app-216501
region: us-east4
```

The connectionName value is in the format [PROJECT_NAME]:[REGION_NAME]:[INSTANCE_NAME].

Initialize the Cloud SQL instance (On Mac)

1. At this point, we may need to get application default creadentials. Otherwise, we will get "could not find default credentials" error when we try to run the Cloud SQL Proxy:

```
Sam.ple-Air:Kubernetes sam.ple$ gcloud auth application-default login
...
Credentials saved to file:
[/Users/sam.ple/.config/gcloud/application_default_credentials.json]
These credentials will be used by any library that requests
Application Default Credentials.
To generate an access token for other uses, run:
  gcloud auth application-default print-access-token
```

Start the Cloud SQL Proxy using the connectionName from the previous step. Linux/Mac OS X

```
./cloud_sql_proxy -instances="[INSTANCE_CONNECTION_NAME]"=tcp:5432
```

Replace [INSTANCE_CONNECTION_NAME] with the value of connectionName that we recorded in the previous step.

```
Sam.ple-Air:Kubernetes sam.ple$ ./cloud_sql_proxy -instances="django-poll-
app-216501:us-east4:polls-instance"=tcp:5432
2018/09/15 12:57:02 Listening on 127.0.0.1:5432 for django-poll-app-
216501:us-east4:polls-instance
2018/09/15 12:57:02 Ready for new connections
```

This step establishes a connection from our local computer (Mac) to our Cloud SQL instance for local testing purposes. Keep the Cloud SQL Proxy running the entire time we test our application locally. So, we may need to open up another local shell terminal.

Create a new Cloud SQL user and database (On Mac)

In this section, we just want to install Postgres.

1. In a separate command-line tab, install the Postgres client.

```
Sam.ple-Air:Kubernetes sam.ple$ brew install postgres
...
To have launchd start postgresql now and restart at login:
  brew services start postgresql
or, if you don't want/need a background service you can just run:
  pg_ctl -D /usr/local/var/postgres start
```

2. Because we don't want/need a background service we can just run:
3. Use the Postgres client or similar program to connect to our instance.
   When prompted, use the root password we configured.

```
psql --host 127.0.0.1 --user postgres --password
```

4. In the earlier section, we've already created the required databases,
   users, and access permissions in our Cloud SQL database.

Creating a service account (On Mac)

We've already created the service account in the earlier section

Configuring the database settings (On Mac)

Now, we want to set environment variables for database access for local
testing on Mac:

```
export DATABASE_USER=<your-database-user>
export DATABASE_PASSWORD=<your-database-password>
Sam.ple-Air:Kubernetes sam.ple$ export DATABASE_USER=khong
Sam.ple-Air:Kubernetes sam.ple$ export DATABASE_PASSWORD=postgres
```

Setting up our GKE configuration (On Mac)

1. This application is represented in a single Kubernetes configuration,
   called polls. In polls.yaml replace <your-project-id> with our project
   ID.

```
kihyuck_hong@cloudshell:~/python-docs-samples/container_engine/django_tutorial
(django-poll-app-216501)$ ls -l
total 7364
-rw-r--r--  1 kihyuck_hong kihyuck_hong        0 Sep 14 21:55 ]
-rwxr-xr-x  1 kihyuck_hong kihyuck_hong  7505002 Sep  7 17:31 cloud_sql_proxy
-rw-r--r--  1 kihyuck_hong kihyuck_hong     1241 Sep 14 21:48 Dockerfile
-rw-r--r--  1 kihyuck_hong kihyuck_hong        0 Sep 14 21:48 __init__.py
-rw-r--r--  1 kihyuck_hong kihyuck_hong      881 Sep 14 21:48 Makefile
-rwxr-xr-x  1 kihyuck_hong kihyuck_hong      825 Sep 14 21:48 manage.py
drwxr-xr-x  2 kihyuck_hong kihyuck_hong     4096 Sep 14 21:48 mysite
drwxr-xr-x  3 kihyuck_hong kihyuck_hong     4096 Sep 14 21:48 polls
-rw-r--r--  1 kihyuck_hong kihyuck_hong     3591 Sep 14 21:48 polls.yaml
-rw-r--r--  1 kihyuck_hong kihyuck_hong     1161 Sep 14 21:48 README.md
-rw-r--r--  1 kihyuck_hong kihyuck_hong       79 Sep 14 21:48 requirements.txt
```

2. In polls.yaml replace <your-cloudsql-connection-string> with the value
   of connectionName outputted from the following command:

```
gcloud beta sql instances describe [YOUR_INSTANCE_NAME]

Sam.ple-Air:django_tutorial sam.ple$ gcloud beta sql instances describe polls-instance
backendType: SECOND_GEN
connectionName: django-poll-app-216501:us-east4:polls-instance
```

```
# [START proxy_container]
- image: b.gcr.io/cloudsql-docker/gce-proxy:1.05
  name: cloudsql-proxy
  command: ["/cloud_sql_proxy", "--dir=/cloudsql",
            "-instances=<your-cloudsql-connection-string>=tcp:5432",
            "-credential_file=/secrets/cloudsql/credentials.json"]
  volumeMounts:
    - name: cloudsql-oauth-credentials
      mountPath: /secrets/cloudsql
      readOnly: true
    - name: ssl-certs
      mountPath: /etc/ssl/certs
    - name: cloudsql
      mountPath: /cloudsql
# [START proxy_container]
- image: b.gcr.io/cloudsql-docker/gce-proxy:1.05
  name: cloudsql-proxy
  command: ["/cloud_sql_proxy", "--dir=/cloudsql",
            "-instances=django-poll-app-216501:us-east4:polls-instance=tcp:5432",
            "-credential_file=/secrets/cloudsql/credentials.json"]
  volumeMounts:
    - name: cloudsql-oauth-credentials
      mountPath: /secrets/cloudsql
      readOnly: true
    - name: ssl-certs
      mountPath: /etc/ssl/certs
    - name: cloudsql
      mountPath: /cloudsql
```

Running the app on our local computer (On Mac)

1. To run the Django app on our local computer (on Mac), we need to set up a Python development environment, including Python, pip, and virtualenv.
2. Sam.ple-Air:django_tutorial sam.ple$ pwd
/Users/sam.ple/Documents/Django/Kubernetes/python-docs-samples/container_engine/django_tutorial

Create an isolated Python environment, and install dependencies:

```
virtualenv venv
source venv/bin/activate
pip install -r requirements.txt
Sam.ple-Air:django_tutorial sam.ple$ python -V
Python 3.7.0
Sam.ple-Air:django_tutorial sam.ple$ pip3 install virtualenv
Sam.ple-Air:django_tutorial sam.ple$ virtualenv venv
Sam.ple-Air:django_tutorial sam.ple$ source venv/bin/activate
(venv) Sam.ple-Air:django_tutorial sam.ple$
```

But I got the following error "mysql_config not found" while "pip install -r requirements.txt":

```
(venv) Sam.ple-Air:django_tutorial sam.ple$ pip install -r requirements.txt
Collecting Django==2.1 (from -r requirements.txt (line 1))
  Downloading
https://files.pythonhosted.org/packages/51/1a/e0ac7886c7123a03814178d7517dc82
2af0fe51a72e1a6bff26153103322/Django-2.1-py3-none-any.whl (7.3MB)
...
Collecting mysqlclient==1.3.13 (from -r requirements.txt (line 2))
...
        raise EnvironmentError("%s not found" % (mysql_config.path,))
    OSError: mysql_config not found
```

Installing "mysql" resolved the issue:

```
(venv) Sam.ple-Air:django_tutorial sam.ple$ brew install mysql

==> Downloading https://homebrew.bintray.com/bottles/mysql-
8.0.12.high_sierra.bottle.tar.gz

################################################################### 100.0%

==> Pouring mysql-8.0.12.high_sierra.bottle.tar.gz

==> /usr/local/Cellar/mysql/8.0.12/bin/mysqld --initialize-insecure --user=sam.ple --
basedir=/usr/local/Cellar/mysql/8.0.12 --datadir=/usr/local/var/mysql --tmpdir=/tmp

...

To connect run:
    mysql -uroot

To have launchd start mysql now and restart at login:
  brew services start mysql

Or, if you don't want/need a background service you can just run:
  mysql.server start
```

3.   We need to give credentials to our environment:

```
(venv) Sam.ple-Air:django_tutorial sam.ple$ export DATABASE_USER=khong

(venv) Sam.ple-Air:django_tutorial sam.ple$ export DATABASE_PASSWORD=postgres
```

4.   Run the Django migrations to set up our models:

```
python manage.py makemigrations

python manage.py makemigrations polls

python manage.py migrate

(venv) Sam.ple-Air:django_tutorial sam.ple$ python manage.py makemigrations

...

Migrations for 'polls':
  polls/migrations/0002_auto_20180915_2309.py
    - Alter field pub_date on question

(venv) Sam.ple-Air:django_tutorial sam.ple$ python manage.py makemigrations polls

...

No changes detected in app 'polls'

(venv) Sam.ple-Air:django_tutorial sam.ple$ python manage.py migrate

...

Operations to perform:
  Apply all migrations: admin, auth, contenttypes, polls, sessions

Running migrations:
  Applying polls.0002_auto_20180915_2309... OK
```

5. Start a local web server:

```
python manage.py runserver
(venv) Sam.ple-Air:django_tutorial sam.ple$ python manage.py runserver
...
Django version 2.1, using settings 'mysite.settings'
Starting development server at http://127.0.0.1:8000/
Quit the server with CONTROL-C.
```

6. Go to http://localhost:8000.

7. Log in to the admin site using the username and password we created when you ran createsuperuser.

We should see a simple webpage with the following text: "Hello, world. You're at the polls index." The sample app pages are delivered by the Django web server running on our computer. When we're ready to move forward, press Ctrl+C to stop the local web server.

Using the Django admin console (On Mac)

1. Create a superuser:

```
python manage.py createsuperuser
(venv) Sam.ple-Air:django_tutorial sam.ple$ python manage.py createsuperuser
...
Username (leave blank to use 'sam.ple'): superuser
Email address: sam.ple@gmail.com
Password:
Password (again):
Superuser created successfully.
```

2. Run the main program:

```
python manage.py runserver
(venv) Sam.ple-Air:django_tutorial sam.ple$ python manage.py runserver
...
Django version 2.1, using settings 'mysite.settings'
Starting development server at http://127.0.0.1:8000/
Quit the server with CONTROL-C.
```

3. In the browser, go to http://localhost:8000/admin.
4. Log in to the admin site using the username and password we created when we ran createsuperuser.

CHAPTER 8: DJANGO DEPLOY VIA KUBERNETES II (GKE)

Deploying the app to GKE

1. When the app is deployed to Google Cloud Platform, it uses the Gunicorn server. Gunicorn doesn't serve static content, so the app uses Cloud Storage to serve static content.

Create a Cloud Storage bucket and make it publicly readable. Replace <your-gcs-bucket> with a bucket name we like. For example, we could use our project ID (django-poll-app-216501) as a bucket name:

```
gsutil mb gs://<your-gcs-bucket>
gsutil defacl set public-read gs://<your-gcs-bucket>
```

```
(venv) Sam.ple-Air:django_tutorial sam.ple$ gsutil mb gs://django-poll-app-216501
Creating gs://django-poll-app-216501/...
(venv) Sam.ple-Air:django_tutorial sam.ple$ gsutil defacl set public-read gs://django-poll-app-216501
Setting default object ACL on gs://django-poll-app-216501/...
```

2. Gather all the static content locally into one folder:

```
python manage.py collectstatic
```

```
(venv) Sam.ple-Air:django_tutorial sam.ple$ python manage.py collectstatic
...
119 static files copied to
'/Users/sam.ple/Documents/Django/Kubernetes/python-docs-
samples/container_engine/django_tutorial/static'.
```

3. Upload the static content to Cloud Storage:

```
gsutil rsync -R static/ gs://<your-gcs-bucket>/static
```

```
(venv) Sam.ple-Air:django_tutorial sam.ple$ gsutil rsync -R static/
gs://django-poll-app-216501/static
```

4. In mysite/settings.py, set the value of STATIC_URL to this URL, replacing <your-gcs-bucket> with your bucket name.

```
http://storage.googleapis.com/<your-gcs-bucket>/static/
...
# Static files (CSS, JavaScript, Images)
# https://docs.djangoproject.com/en/1.8/howto/static-files/
# [START staticurl]
STATIC_URL = '/static/'
STATIC_URL = 'https://storage.googleapis.com/django-poll-app-216501/static/'
# [END staticurl]
```

5. To initialize GKE, go to the GCP Console. Wait for the "Kubernetes Engine is getting ready.

This may take a minute or more" message to disappear.

6. Create a GKE cluster:

```
# [START kubernetes_deployment]
apiVersion: extensions/v1beta1
kind: Deployment
metadata:
  name: polls
  labels:
    app: polls
spec:
  replicas: 3
  template:
    metadata:
      labels:
        app: polls
    spec:
      containers:
      - name: polls-app
        # Replace  with your project ID or use `make template`
        image: gcr.io//polls
        # This setting makes nodes pull the docker image every time before
        # starting the pod. This is useful when debugging, but should be turned
        # off in production.
        imagePullPolicy: Always
        env:
            # [START cloudsql_secrets]
          - name: DATABASE_USER
            valueFrom:
              secretKeyRef:
                name: cloudsql
                key: username
          - name: DATABASE_PASSWORD
            valueFrom:
              secretKeyRef:
                name: cloudsql
                key: password
          # [END cloudsql_secrets]
        ports:
        - containerPort: 8080
```

7. After the cluster is created, use the kubectl command-line tool, which is integrated with the gcloud tool, to interact with our GKE cluster. Because gcloud and kubectl are separate tools, make sure kubectl is configured to interact with the right cluster.

After creating our cluster, we need to get authentication credentials to interact with the cluster. To authenticate for the cluster, run the following command:

```
gcloud container clusters get-credentials CLUSTER_NAME --zone "us-east4-c"
```

This command configures kubectl to use the cluster we created.

```
(venv) Sam.ple-Air:django_tutorial sam.ple$ gcloud container clusters get-credentials
polls --zone us-east4-c --project django-poll-app-216501
Fetching cluster endpoint and auth data.
kubeconfig entry generated for polls.
```

8. We need several secrets to enable our GKE app to connect with our Cloud SQL instance. One is required for instance-level access (connection), while the other two are required for database access.

The two Secrets to enable our Kubernetes Engine application to access the data in our Cloud SQL instance are:

a) The cloudsql-instance-credentials Secret contains the service account.

b) The cloudsql-db-credentials Secret provides the database user account and password.

Create these Secrets:

1. To create the secret for instance-level access, provide the location of the key we downloaded when we created our service account:

```
kubectl create secret generic cloudsql-oauth-credentials --from-
file=credentials.json=[PROXY_KEY_FILE_PATH]|
```

```
(venv) Sam.ple-Air:django_tutorial sam.ple$ kubectl create secret generic
cloudsql-oauth-credentials --from-
file=credentials.json=/Users/sam.ple/Documents/Django/Kubernetes/django-poll-
app-216501-f4ffa0d2f930.json
secret "cloudsql-oauth-credentials" created
```

Initailly, I got this error: "The connection to the server localhost:8080 was refused - did you specify the right host or port?"
This indicates that kubectl is not properly configured.
To check if kubectl is properly configured by getting the cluster state:

```
$ kubectl cluster-info
```

If we see a URL response, kubectl is correctly configured to access our cluster. But if we see a message similar to the above, kubectl is not correctly configured or not able to connect to a Kubernetes cluster.
Somehow, either minikube has been stopped or uninstalled. So, I had to reinstall and start it, and everything starts working fine.

```
$ curl -Lo minikube
https://storage.googleapis.com/minikube/releases/v0.28.2/minikube-darwin-
amd64 && chmod +x minikube && sudo mv minikube /usr/local/bin/

$ minikube start
```

2. Create the secrets needed for database access:

```
kubectl create secret generic cloudsql --from-
literal=username=[PROXY_USERNAME] --from-literal=password=[PASSWORD]

(venv) Sam.ple-Air:django_tutorial sam.ple$ kubectl create secret generic
cloudsql --from-literal=username=khong --from-literal=password=postgres

secret "cloudsql" created
```

9. Retrieve the public Docker image for the Cloud SQL proxy.

```
docker pull b.gcr.io/cloudsql-docker/gce-proxy:1.05

(venv) Sam.ple-Air:django_tutorial sam.ple$ docker pull b.gcr.io/cloudsql-
docker/gce-proxy:1.05
```

10. Build a Docker image, replacing <your-project-id> with your project
    ID.

```
docker build -t gcr.io/<your-project-id>/polls .

(venv) Sam.ple-Air:django_tutorial sam.ple$ docker build -t gcr.io/django-poll-app-
216501/polls .

...

Successfully built 4687297fcf19

Successfully tagged gcr.io/django-poll-app-216501/polls:latest
```

11. Configure docker to use gcloud as a credential helper, so that we can
    push the image to Google Container Registry:

```
gcloud auth configure-docker

(venv) Sam.ple-Air:django_tutorial sam.ple$ gcloud auth configure-docker

The following settings will be added to your Docker config file

located at [/Users/sam.ple/.docker/config.json]:

 {
  "credHelpers": {
    "gcr.io": "gcloud",
    "us.gcr.io": "gcloud",
    "eu.gcr.io": "gcloud",
    "asia.gcr.io": "gcloud",
    "staging-k8s.gcr.io": "gcloud",
    "marketplace.gcr.io": "gcloud"
  }
}

Do you want to continue (Y/n)?  Y

Docker configuration file updated.
```

12. Push the Docker image. Replace <your-project-id> with your project ID.

```
docker push gcr.io/<your-project-id>/polls|
```

```
(venv) Sam.ple-Air:django_tutorial sam.ple$ docker push gcr.io/django-
poll-app-216501/polls|
```

Note: This command requires write access to Cloud Storage. If we run this tutorial on a Compute Engine instance, our access to Cloud Storage might be read-only. To get write access, create a service account and use the service account to authenticate on our instance.

13. Create the GKE resource:

```
kubectl create -f polls.yaml
```

```
(venv) Sam.ple-Air:django_tutorial sam.ple$ kubectl create -f polls.yaml
deployment "polls" created
service "polls" created
```

14. After the resources are created, there should be three polls pods on the cluster. Check the status of the pods:

kubectl get pods

```
(venv) Kihyucks-Air:django_tutorial kihyuckhong$ kubectl get pods
NAME                   READY    STATUS             RESTARTS    AGE
polls-c648d749d-6b2w7  0/2      ContainerCreating  0           16s
polls-c648d749d-mzq72  0/2      ContainerCreating  0           16s
polls-c648d749d-t67b2  0/2      ContainerCreating  0           16s

(venv) Kihyucks-Air:django_tutorial kihyuckhong$ kubectl get pods
NAME                   READY    STATUS    RESTARTS    AGE
polls-c648d749d-6b2w7  2/2      Running   0           7m
polls-c648d749d-mzq72  2/2      Running   0           7m
polls-c648d749d-t67b2  2/2      Running   0           7m
```

Wait a few minutes for the pod statuses to turn to Running.

Managed pods

Revision	Name ∧	Status	Restarts
1	polls-c648d749d-6b2w7	Running	0
1	polls-c648d749d-mzq72	Running	0
1	polls-c648d749d-t67b2	Running	0

If the pods are not ready or if we see restarts, we can get the logs for a particular pod to figure out the issue:

```
kubectl logs <your-pod-id>
```

15.

```
(venv) Kihyucks-Air:django_tutorial kihyuckhong$ kubectl cluster-info

Kubernetes master is running at https://35.188.242.239

GLBCDefaultBackend is running at https://35.188.242.239/api/v1/namespaces/kube-system/services/default-http-backend:http/proxy

Heapster is running at https://35.188.242.239/api/v1/namespaces/kube-system/services/heapster/proxy

KubeDNS is running at https://35.188.242.239/api/v1/namespaces/kube-system/services/kube-dns:dns/proxy

kubernetes-dashboard is running at https://35.188.242.239/api/v1/namespaces/kube-system/services/https:kubernetes-dashboard:/proxy

Metrics-server is running at https://35.188.242.239/api/v1/namespaces/kube-system/services/https:metrics-server:/proxy
```

App running in GCP

After the pods are ready, we can get the public IP address of the load balancer:

```
(venv) Kihyucks-Air:django_tutorial kihyuckhong$ kubectl get services polls
NAME     TYPE           CLUSTER-IP      EXTERNAL-IP     PORT(S)        AGE
polls    LoadBalancer   10.47.247.135   35.188.234.3    80:32279/TCP   13m
```

Navigate to the EXTERNAL-IP address in our browser to see the Django basic landing page and access the admin console.

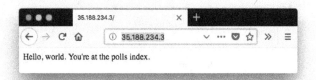